Sacagawea

A Buddy Book
by
Sarah Tieck

ABDO
Publishing Company

VISIT US AT

www.abdopublishing.com

Published by ABDO Publishing Company, 4940 Viking Drive, Suite 622, Edina, Minnesota 55435. Copyright © 2007 by Abdo Consulting Group, Inc. International copyrights reserved in all countries. No part of this book may be reproduced in any form without written permission from the publisher.

Printed in the United States.

Contributing Editor: Michael P. Goecke
Graphic Design: Jane Halbert
Cover Photograph: Library of Congress
Interior Photographs/Illustrations: Hulton Archives, Library of Congress, North Wind, Photodisc

Library of Congress Cataloging-in-Publication Data

Tieck, Sarah, 1976–
   Sacagawea / Sarah Tieck.
      p. cm. — (First biographies. Set V.)
   Includes index.
   ISBN 10 1-59679-789-4
   ISBN 13 978-1-59679-789-5
   1. Sacagawea—Juvenile literature. 2. Shoshone women—Biography—Juvenile literature. 3. Shoshone Indians—Juvenile literature. 4. Lewis and Clark Expedition (1804-1806)—Juvenile literature. I. Title II. Series: Tieck, Sarah, 1976- . First biographies. Set V.

F592.7.S123T54 2006
978.00497'45740092—dc22
                                              2005031972

Table Of Contents

Who Is Sacagawea?

Sacagawea (sa-kuh-ga-WEE-uh) was a famous Native American.

Sacagawea lived in the United States more than 200 years ago. At that time, the West was a great wilderness. Back then, many different Native American tribes lived on this land. Nobody else knew much about the area.

Meriwether Lewis and William Clark explored the United States in the early 1800s. Sacagawea helped them. She joined the explorers when they arrived in North Dakota. She traveled with them all the way to the Pacific Ocean and back. Sacagawea helped the United States grow into a strong country.

William Clark and Meriwether Lewis

A Shoshone Girl

Sacagawea was born around 1787. Some people know her as Sacajawea or Sakakawea. Sacagawea means "Bird Woman."

Sacagawea was part of a Shoshone tribe. Her tribe lived in what is now Idaho. Some people say Sacagawea's father was a leader of the Shoshone tribe.

North Dakota and Idaho are in the United States of America.

Sacagawea's tribe lived near the Rocky Mountains. As a girl, Sacagawea learned to find roots and berries to eat. She also learned about the land around her home.

Growing Up

When Sacagawea was about 12 years old, she was taken from her Shoshone family by the Hidatsa tribe. The Hidatsa lived in what is now North Dakota. Sacagawea went to live with them in their village.

A drawing of Sacagawea.

When she was about 16, Sacagawea married a French-Canadian fur trader. His name was Toussaint Charbonneau. He married Sacagawea in the winter of 1804.

A monument of Sacagawea and her son.

Sacagawea and Toussaint's son was born on February 11, 1805. They named him Jean-Baptiste Charbonneau. He was sometimes called "Pomp."

Exploring The West

In 1804, Meriwether Lewis and William Clark arrived at the Hidatsa-Mandan villages. Lewis and Clark were famous American explorers. They were on a trip, or expedition, to explore the western United States.

A view of a Mandan village.

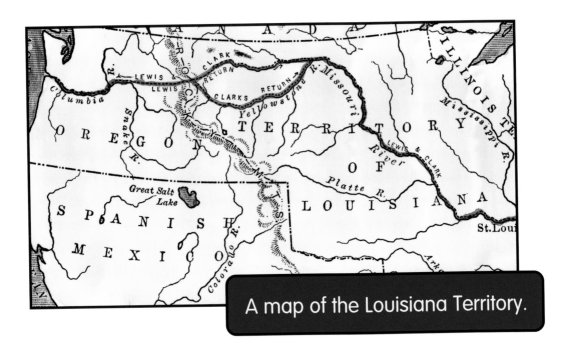

A map of the Louisiana Territory.

President Thomas Jefferson called Lewis and Clark's group the "Corps of Discovery." The Corps of Discovery was exploring the Louisiana Territory and the Northwest. Most people didn't know much about this area.

In November 1804, Lewis and Clark built a fort near the Native American villages. It was called Fort Mandan. Toussaint and Sacagawea met Lewis and Clark there.

A view of Fort Mandan today.

Sacagawea knew a lot about the West. Lewis and Clark knew that Sacagawea could help them. They asked Toussaint and Sacagawea to join their expedition. Toussaint and Sacagawea would be interpreters.

Sacagawea interprets for Lewis and Clark.

Lewis and Clark left Fort Mandan in April 1805. Toussaint and Sacagawea went, too. They brought Pomp with them. He was just two months old. Sacagawea carried him on her back. She and Pomp showed the other Native Americans that the Corps of Discovery wanted peace.

A Brave Explorer

The trip through the wilderness was very hard. Sacagawea helped teach the explorers. She found roots and fruit for the men to eat. She helped to guide the expedition to the Pacific Ocean. People said she was brave, quick, and helpful.

A view of Lewis and Clark Trail in Washington State.

The Corps of Discovery sailed in special boats. One type of boat was a pirogue. Pirogues are like canoes. They helped carry people and supplies. Some of these supplies were foods, medicines, presents for Native Americans, tools, and guns. These supplies were very important.

On May 14, 1805, the pirogue Sacagawea and Pomp were riding in tipped because of the wind. It started to fill with water. Many of the supplies fell out.

Sacagawea made sure that Pomp was safe on her back. Then, she began to put the supplies that had fallen into the water back into her boat. She stopped them from floating away.

Two things Sacagawea saved were the journals of Lewis and Clark. The explorers were very grateful for this. The journals contained notes and drawings from the expedition. There were many stories about Sacagawea in the journals, too.

A Special Reunion

In August 1805, the Corps of Discovery was going to cross the Bitterroot Mountains. These mountains are in the northern Rockies. Lewis and Clark knew that this was a dangerous trip. They would need horses.

The Lewis and Clark Trail goes over Lolo Pass. It is in the Bitterroot Mountains of Montana.

They wanted to trade with the Shoshone people for horses. They knew Sacagawea could help. She spoke the Shoshone language and could translate for them.

Lewis and Clark met many Native Americans.

Lewis and Clark found a Shoshone tribe. The chief's name was Chief Cameahwait. Sacagawea asked if he would trade for horses. As Sacagawea spoke with Chief Cameahwait, she

Lewis and Clark greet Chief Cameahwait.

realized he was her brother. She hadn't seen him for many years. They were very happy to see each other.

Chief Cameahwait said he would help Sacagawea's friends. He gave them horses. Sacagawea could have stayed with the tribe. But, she wanted to finish the journey with Lewis and Clark. She thanked her brother and continued on to the Pacific Ocean with the explorers. On November 7, 1805, the explorers' journals said they saw the Pacific Ocean for the first time.

A view of the Pacific Ocean.

Home Again

On August 14, 1806, the Corps of Discovery arrived back at the Hidatsa-Mandan villages. Sacagawea, Toussaint, and Pomp said good-bye to Lewis and Clark. Toussaint was given land and $500.33 for helping the explorers.

Sacagawea and her family made a home in North Dakota. They also traveled. In 1812, Sacagawea had another child. She and Toussaint named their daughter Lisette Charbonneau.

Sacagawea, Pomp, and Toussaint.

Later that year, Sacagawea got very sick. She had a bad fever. She died in December 1812. She was about 25 years old.

There is a legend that says Sacagawea did not die in 1812. Some people believe she lived to be very old. No one knows for sure what happened. Many people believe she did die young, though. This is because William Clark made a note on a list of the explorers that said Sacagawea died in 1812. Also, he took care of Lisette and Pomp after Sacagawea died.

Honoring Sacagawea

Today, Sacagawea is honored for helping Lewis and Clark. She was very brave and taught the explorers many things.

There is a river in Montana named for Sacagawea. Also, there are many monuments and statues to honor her. There is even a coin with a picture of Sacagawea on it.

Sacagawea is pictured on the dollar coin.

A statue of Lewis and Clark with Sacagawea in Charlottesville, Virginia.

29

Important Dates

1787 Sacagawea is born around this time. No one knows the exact date.

1800 Around this time, Sacagawea is taken from the Shoshones. She goes to live in the Hidatsa villages.

1804 Sacagawea marries Toussaint Charbonneau. He is a French-Canadian fur trader.

Winter 1804 to 1805 Meriwether Lewis and William Clark stop near the Hidatsa-Mandan villages. They build Fort Mandan and stay there for the winter. Toussaint and Sacagawea join the Corps of Discovery.

February 1805 Sacagawea gives birth to a son. His name is Jean-Baptiste Charbonneau.

April 1805 Sacagawea leaves Fort Mandan with the Corps of Discovery.

August 1805 The Corps of Discovery meets members of the Shoshone Native American tribe. Chief Cameahwait is Sacagawea's brother.

August 1806 The Corps of Discovery finishes its exploration. Sacagawea and her family return to North Dakota.

1812 Sacagawea gives birth to a daughter. Her name is Lisette Charbonneau.

December 1812 Sacagawea dies.

Important Words

expedition a trip to find something new.

explorers people who closely look at something new.

interpreters people who explain the meaning of words in another language.

Louisiana Territory a big piece of land the United States bought from France in 1803.

Native Americans the very first people who lived in America.

translate to explain the meaning of words of a different language.

tribe a group of Native Americans who live together.

wilderness wild land where very few people live.

Web Sites

To learn more about Sacagawea, visit ABDO Publishing Company on the World Wide Web. Web site links about Sacagawea are featured on our Book Links page. These links are routinely monitored and updated to provide the most current information available.

www.abdopublishing.com

Index